Words, Images & Imagina

Poems Watercolour Phot

Andrew Pratt

Dedicated to Melody, Madeleine, Isaac & Reuben

Mystery and wonder,
love and compassion have freedom
when we recognise that
no 'religious' creed can ever be fixed or final.
Then love can encompass those we have,
in our wisdom,
deemed to be beyond love
even if our scripture and tradition
seem to tell us otherwise.

1

Words, Images and Imagination
Copyright @ (Andrew Pratt 2020)

ISBN: 97-178456-740-8
Paperback

First published 2020 by UPFRONT PUBLISHING
Peterborough, England.

An environmentally friendly book printed and bound in England
by www.printondemand-worldwide.com

Preface

I was born in a small guest house within four hundred yards of the sea in Paignton in Devon, which accounts for the marine strands which weave through this collection, surfacing every so often.

An inspiration for the collection came when, putting together an item for ArtServe magazine, I returned to a hymn which had itself been inspired by Leonard Cohen's song Suzanne. In it he sings, 'Jesus was a sailor'. The article was accompanied by one of my water colours and the seeds of words, images and imagination had been sown. This book is the natural evolution of the experiment of associating these threads. It was compiled during the 2020 COVID-19 pandemic, though the material is not all directly related to the this. Lockdown offered time for the volume to be put together.

I have been writing hymns since 1979 and have over 1500 in copyright with Stainer & Bell Ltd who have produced four collections of my texts. I have been taking photographs on and off since the late 1950s, beginning around the age of 10. My watercolour painting began while I was studying Marine Biology in North Wales in 1970, writing poetry at the same time. My first publication of a poem was in a college magazine in 1972 while training as a teacher.

CONTENTS

Torbay – Thatcher Rock

ALWAYS THE SEA

The suck of surf through shingle

The suck of surf through shingle sounds
as though the ocean has breath,
heaves and leaves,

pulls up, draws out,
for a second is still,

until the coruscating brilliance of moonlight shines,
is gone,
shattered in a thousand shards,

then falling back in peace as,

like old Galilee, is dark and still
to the echo of the very voice of God.

Menai Sunset

The sea is mill-pond still

The sea is mill-pond still
and nothing stirs.
The bow cuts through the sullen sea
and foam is left
trailing where we came.

Movement's breeze
cools and calms
as the warm of the day
seeps away
and indigo clothes the sky.

The last cinders of sunlight are quenched
and through the darkened silence,
hand in hand,
we go below together...

the sullen sea – these sullen waters?

The Mill-Pond Sea

Cathartic shining chaos

Cathartic shining chaos
each rivulet or storm,
the elements of nature
that contravene the norm;

brutality and beauty,
each savage tooth and claw,
each standing stone or sunset,
will warm our hearts with awe.

Bright moonlight slaking ripples
across the mid-night lake,
as leaves translate to stipples
each cinematic take;

the picture framed and mounted,
the photograph in view,
has simply, now, enchanted
the many, and the few.

RELATIONSHIPS

To make a covenant

To make a covenant
is more than simply words.
Your woven lives and living love
will make your vows more real.

The gravity of love
makes falling easy,
but holding on
and keeping close…

No parachute
but care to break
indifference
can make the fall
precarious.

So love
and never take for granted
all that you are given,
nor all you have to give.

Yes love,
and love,
and love again,
through all the life you live.

As light fades

As light fades,
as tears deride
and love,

an ebbing tide

recedes.

Shingle dries in sun…

passion cooled
is hard as rock.

Passion cooled…

The grain of timber

The grain of timber,
hewn and carved,
polished,
reveals a hidden beauty.

And eyes discern a pattern,
a purpose,
in quiet clouds and crashing waves,
the force of wind,
the hush of turning tide.

When once you met
you did not know what lay ahead.

Two strangers
on the threshold of
discovery,
you carved and delved,
discerned and delighted
in accents of character,
gentle and fierce,
echoes of love
that others could not see.

Surprised by joy
you found in
companionship
the friendship
that transcends difficulty
and delights
in the other's good.

The hush of turning tide

It could have been a cosy Armageddon

When arguments are brewing we don't notice,
it seems that tension builds with every word,
we say things while not hearing one another,
like children in a playground, quite absurd!

It could have been a cosy Armageddon,
the words had seemed innocuous and bland,
yet hidden in each phrase, each idle sentence,
were thoughts designed to undermine each stand.

If we could simply seek a gracious outcome
when others hurt and harass, fault or harm,
a look inspired by love could turn the tables,
could echo hidden need, befriend, disarm.

Meant to be

"Meant to be",
you said.
Two lives
spinning
independently
through the firmament.
Cosmic aeons in preparation.
Chance collisions
in time and space.
Moulded by experience
and circumstance.

So many
possibilities …
impossibilities,
so many turnings
missed,
or taken,
bringing you to this day.

And no cliché,
or well-worn rhyme,
can formulate,
discern,
define
the beauty of your
love.

"Meant to be",
you said.
"Meant to be."

All my life I've made acquaintances*

All my life I've made acquaintances
not friends,
a varied tapestry of faces,
none permanent,
born and dying.

Parents gave me birth,
both now dead.
Child born
and laid to rest.
One human love remains constant,
always constant since we met,
yet even she will die.

And if I survive,
at the ultimate parting of the ways,
I will be alone.

Left again to my earliest
memories,
to the rising of the sun
and its setting;
to waxing of the moon
and its waning;
the movement of the waters,
the crashing of the waves,
the constancy of stars;
to the generation of my faith.

In this dynamic patchwork
I find my safety,
lodge securely;
and so,
in death,
I will return again
to the friendly sea
and the sky.

*Originally published in Poppies and
Snowdrops

20

The friendly sea

PERSPECTIVES

Our empty myths and promises

Our empty myths and promises:
less comfort? More disturb!

When met with stark reality
we greet the honest truth:
that news is false,
and those who echo pious words,
that "death is nothing, just a hoax"
are greeted where, some six feet deep,
a body dead, and cold and still
is proof to make us weep.

And you who tell immortal tales
admit to me now, this is a lie,
if what you mean is earthly life.

But if you boast of scripture's truth,
remember that Christ died,
entombed, and left for dead,

And only now,
in later years,
inspires some act,
remembrance,

in water, wine and bread.

In wine and bread

Freedom*

The world sees freedom like elastic,
only so far and not too far…

Say what you like, but don't say that.
Go where you will, but don't go there.

Like fish in a net we can only swim as far
as the mesh of culture,
or religion,
or convention will allow.

Go to the land of God's promise
but don't expect a welcome.

Living there, blessed, in a
land of milk and honey,
know this,

that God can change her
mind,
can gender shift, can alter
rule and practise,

can counter expectation at a
whim...

in the name of LOVE...

*Commissioned by the Joint Public Issues Team
of the UK Churches

Must this clerical obsession

Must this clerical obsession
ultimately break us,
we who minister
within constraints of creed,
which hobble intellect
and cripple reason?

We no longer seek
or probe
but vainly,
blindly,
follow sightless guides
gone before.

TIME

Persephone

Persephone, they said, delved deep
through winter's scold.
The leaves of autumn fell, condemned to mould,
a burial, deep, seemed permanent and cold.

And so it was till snow had fallen,
frosted soil had hardened into stone,
a frozen, hurtful bed,
where all seemed dark and dead.

Incomprehensibly, some life still lurked
within this frigid earth,
and, hidden still, green shoots would come to birth.

And so, they said, reflecting, Persephone would rise,
beneath the early skies of lengthening days.
Experience led this hope,
but other days would sound a different song.

Divine interpretation sees,
in nature, re-creation,
an annual resurrection,
a seasonal response
to winter's dereliction.
And as the seasons turn
a spirit still may burn,
and breath may move and breathe,
a song may ring where
cold and void and chaos rule,
to usher in God's Spring.

This frigid earth

Mouldy old log at the turning of the year

Mouldy old log at the turning of the year,
once green,
now dead,
lacking sap.

Sad year passing,
gone,
dead.

Watch the turning,
burning of the season,
till white ash snow,
melting brings life,
again.

Not immortality
for that mouldy old log at the turning
of the year
is dead.

But new life springs fresh
forcing through cracked,
raw, hardened earth,
starting again,

and that is what we, also,
should do…on and on…season after
season…starting anew.

Mouldy old log

29

The carousel goes round and round

The carousel goes round and round,
life's turning seems to have no end.
Forever moments flash,
reviving memories.
Blind to the cacophony,
deaf to the sight,
we lack comprehension,
insensate to any progression.

And so years unfold
their monotonous repetition,
until some urgent cataclysm
shatters the ringing,
clang of life and is changed forever.

Now we treasure
the flight of the arrow
from bow-bend
to ultimate collision,
grasping the fact that birth
has set our lives to trace
beyond the spin of youth,
its inevitable finite path.

And ultimately death will have
dominion,
the arrow in full flèche
parsing the last evening sky,
flashing to oblivion.

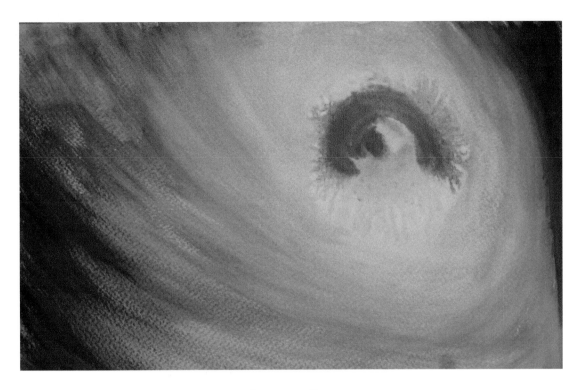

Incarnation

FUTURES

Firm foundations shift and crumble

Firm foundations shift and crumble,
certain fact was writ in sand,
tides have swept what we thought certain,
now we grope to understand.
Calculations once computed
answers we could count as sure,
expectations prove unfounded,
everything is insecure.

In the past we turned to 'God-head',
'fortress', 'shield', 'foundation', 'tower';
images that now seem dated,
insubstantial in this hour.
Is this time to shift our focus,
in admission we are wrong,
set aside our misconceptions,
learn to sing a different song?

Hope no longer in theconstruct
of some super-human thought,
praised with human incantation
built on 'faith' imposed or caught?

Time perusing 'sacred' scripture
written in another age,
now seems wasted in this moment
as we mount this final stage?

Can we pause, admit to falsehood,
own that much is in our hands,
notes once sung that seemed discordant
followed patterns we command?

If the mists of our confusion
are to clear, we need to grasp
that the answer to illusion
rests in facts known from our past:
Every life that has existed
had a span begun in birth.
Every life is always finite
ending at some point on earth.

All we know is bound by limits,
though we might extend or cure,
length of life, or human frailty,
death is certain, still secure.
As a consequence, rethinking
ought to be an urgent task,
working out a way of living,
facing truth without a mask.

Putting off the cloak of hatred,
breaking walls
we thought made safe,
speaking honest,
gracious phrases,
not the words that hurt or chafe;

find new ways of living, loving,
setting us a way ahead,
food for all and wealth for sharing,
end of war and death of dread,
till we hold all things in common,
others valued and affirmed,
knowing God within, around us,
love of neighbour
proved,
confirmed.

Firm foundations

Who will break the spokes today?*

And who will break the spokes today?
Experience civilises us… doesn't it?
Language helps negotiation.
Jaw-jaw, not war-war.

The wheels of government turn, unseen.
Doors close on the truth,
untruth behind the blinds…aptly named.

And rust grows, still the rust gnaws,
the squeals heard
are not really the cries of hungry children.
There is no hunger, do look the other way.

You cannot see the greed and want of power.

We have no intention to dominate and crush.
We must use your gifts carefully
sure not to share with those
who might misuse or waste.

Not corruption, this is care,
We must not perpetuate old ills
of profligacy.

And out of sight,
Beyond check or balance,
the wheels turn,
and who will break the spokes
today?

Who will spoke the
wheel…now?
Spin spanners in the works?

Who will scatter now the proud
in the imagination of their
hearts?

Well who? Just who?

* Dietrich Bonhoeffer, suggested that we ought
not simply to bind up those run over by the
wheel of politics, but to break the wheel itself.

After the vote

Already reaping expectations
of the choices we have made,
children wait in sundry mangers.

Families walking into exile
still unwelcome at our shore,
those not drowned beneath a sullen sea…

Does some Herod wait,
still scheming,
keeping up the vile pretence –
waiting for a celebration…
planning yet another dawn?

Magi stand in the wings
of an infant's play
bearing false gifts,
guilt covered cardboard boxes,
rich perfume to mask stale corruption.

Yet, out of this pantomime
may yet emerge
a deeper understanding...

Will today's innocents survive the
devastations of power, politics and
greed?

Go home by another way?

Another way?

CONFLICT

*So easy now to judge**

So easy now to judge:
that one was right,
another wrong.

But we were never there
in the narrow trench
or corridor of power.
We never heard the thunder's fire,
nor found ourselves
strung up upon the wire.
We never had to make that bleak decision
consigning one to death,
another to derision.

Our innocence is born of inexperience,
our wisdom consummated in our ignorance.
And if the clocks turned back,
were we to tread where men,

now dead,
once walked,
would we be just as speedy
to deride,
or criticise the ones we said
once lied?

Dear God,
give generosity of thought
to read the pages
history have wrought;
to look with eyes of grace
into that time,
to fathom truth and reason
in that jagged, harrowed
rhyme.
Then let our lines
not ridicule the dead,
for, but for grace,
we might repeat their acts,
yes, but for grace,
we might yet taste their dread.

*Written in 2014 for the Centenary of World War One

No armistice*

No armistice
and every day a memory,
not remembrance.
Survival's guilt hangs heavy
like a shroud.

The frightened eyes,
the failing breath,
the flailing limbs,
I will never forget.
Never forget.

Decades pass,
yet nothing fades,
vivid as yesterday
the violence,
the carnage,
flamed on the retina
of my mind.

I hold his hand,
hear his voice,
he slips away,
is,
yet is no more,

And
at the going down of the sun
and in every blazing,
blinding moment
I will remember him.
God where is your victory?
Death, I feel your sting.
Christ! …
hold me.

* Inspired by the recollection of a soldier
from the First World War who told the story
of holding the hand of his dying friend
(From: Poppies and Snowdrops)

*For VE Day**

They sent him home, a broken man,
each nerve and sinew torn or strained
and what was celebrated then
he recognised as little gained.

The trauma of that noise and strife,
the shattered buildings, tear torn lives,
with stunned, dismembered memories,
and, though he struggled, each survives.

The shell-shocked
post-traumatic stress,
his past so vivid, sharpened, bright,
has left him stumbling
through a void,
toward a mist enshrouded night.

And now as we look back this day,
into a past that some have known,
may we revere the ones we see,
and recognise the grief they own.

And deeper truths
must still be learned:
that no dispute is worth a life,
that peace and justice,
kindness, love,
must bring an end to earthly strife.

*For my Father

40

Triptych

DECEPTION

Hard to complain

Hard to complain,
sounds churlish…
presents and tinsel
adorn and clutter,
in "tales of old" the candles gutter.

Replete from the feast,
sleepy,
why should I moan?
Nor yet lament,
cry out:
"my God, my God…why are we forsaking them?"

Washed by a tsunami,
shaken by earthquakes,
threatened by fire, dust, lava.

And our compassion rises,
as soon is dissipated.

Yet closer, on our shores,
tiny rubber dinghies bring
a "threatening" cargo of
migrant people who,
so says the lie, "present a
crisis".

Voices are strident or silent,
and the slaughter
of the innocents
passes,
largely unremarked,
in our churches.

Yet still they come.

And we, anything but innocent,
"standby to repel boarders"
instead of asking
"why do they come?"
And facing with honesty the truth
that people do not run into danger
unless running from something worse?

This cruel sea

Avoiding eye contact, I draw patterns in wet sand.
And lamenting, I weep,
"my God, my God…why are we forsaking them?

In hidden caves of self-deception

In hidden caves of self-deception
no one knows the horrors that we fear.
Passing by we look away.
Someone might otherwise notice our interest.
To this we will not admit.
But darkness covers us.

Hidden we hide those longings.
Deep buried thoughts are locked
in the chambers of our dreams.

Some later memoir might admit
to adolescent fantasies,
But, for now I turn and walk the other way,
kidding myself that a thousand eyes
are blind to all I know,
will not admit.

Longing for the freedom*

Longing for the freedom –
we've been praying all the way -
longing for the dawning of our Lord's eternal day,
waiting on the promises of all God has to say,
slaves of Egypt's money game –
they'll win at every play.

Waiting for deliverance
to break the wheels of power,
Wheels that crush the weakest,
push them lower hour by hour,
while these monuments are rising
in the land beside the Nile,
slaves are marching, slaves are marching ...
but we have their names on file.

Such an enigmatic story
it will twist and turn and bend
and we'll wonder as we wander
will it ever have an end?

Waters part
and freedom beckons
and it seems
that we'll be free,
plagues behind
and Pharaoh blighted,
chasing,
cast into the sea.

Such a sudden exaltation,
the path ahead was wide
as the waters
flooded inward –
cataclysmic,
drowning tide.
But the memory is triumphant,
we're unworried
by the death
of these powerful men
and horses
as they draw
their final breath.

And the winning side
move onward,
they were not to know how long
they would wander in this desert,
and lament this desert song.
Better flesh pots they were leaving,
better hunger of the past
as their joy was soon frustrated
for this wilderness would last.
In the end was their beginning
in a tragic, promised land,
gifted to them by the God-head
as their scriptures understand.

In a future would be exile,
then return, a temple built.
Then a Saviour? Or a scapegoat
to assuage a nation's guilt?
But the history they set turning
through millennia still spins,

* Commissioned by the Joint Public Issues Team
of the UK Churches

And human beings suffer
whenever someone wins.

Who will welcome, who will harbour
wandering migrants such as these?

While history has a habit of
repeating human fault,
now the seas, not praise, are rising,
nature starting its assault.
Like Canute our rulers, blinded,
build defences that can't stand
up against creation's forces
building castles in the sand;
while another torture threatens,
melting ice and rising seas:
those bereft of home and comfort
run beset by death's disease.
And the question echoes hollow,
echoes in our ears again:

Who will welcome, who will harbour
wandering migrants such as these?

Good Friday

DEATH

Hopelessness

Uncertainty pleads for reassurance.

Words drop like feathers
drift and float
as if to gloat as we reach,
then over-reach,
to grasp at the impossible gift –

as a bird might drift and slide
losing footing on a thermal's edge,
falling
interminably.

The shattered bones,
the scattered feathers
seem to be
the inevitable conclusion of this wild sortie –

"a wing and a prayer",
it once was said.

But what,

when wings bend and bones
break before the wind,
what then,

if prayer is but
an ineffectual pick-axe
pummelling a cloud;
a scythe against snow,

and hope all melts around us?

Peregrine

This festive flight…

the Spirit offers wings
to every thought and prayer that ever was.

This soaring elegance
is all of God
yet brightly vicious
tearing pinions from its prey.

Falling from the sky the devil's minion,
messenger of doom hurtles,
falls,
halts within a footfall of the soil
and lifts that rodent,
eyes afire with fear
that feels its final breath as lifted heavenward...

a final flight.

* In tribute to David Attenborough's reading of The Peregrine by J.A. Baker on BBC Sounds

49

There's no suspicion

There's no suspicion
round this present death,
just total loss
and lingering wilderness.

The way my feet had passed,
the path I walked,
is overgrown,
entangled,
crossed
and barred.

Where can I go?
No way,
no way is clear…

Dull thumped the hull
to the jetty's edge.
Then gone, lost in mist.

The bell buoy clanged.
Water lapped.
A shout.
The dark swell
consumed the evidence.
Nothing.
No one found.
Rough night that was.

But two dead to
remember it.

Galvanised steel batted back rain,
making sense as much as convoluted conversation.
Darkness battered down hatches,
sail set, hawsers rang to the coarse whip of steel.

Shipwreck

MEMORY AND HOPE

What are the memories we can share?

What are the memories we can share
when nothing comes to mind?
What are the hopes that lift us up
to ride beyond this storm?

How can we thank an absent God,
for that is how it feels?

Come to our emptiness and fear
and make your presence real.

Come to the midst of our distress,
"abide with me" we sing,
and as we sing the tears may fall
and empty sadness ring.

Stay with us God,
if you can hear a solitary cry.
Stay with us till the storm is past,
stay if we live or die.

Take us away into the night,
of bleakest dark despair.
Stand with us in the blinding sun
and shield our eyes from fear.

Wherever life may weave or wind,
walk with us all the way.
Hold us in love that will not fade
or simply drift away.

And go with the one we love and
leave,
still keep her in your care.
This is our prayer, O God we cry,
don't leave us in despair.

The jagged edge of memory

The jagged edge of memory,
the scars of open love,
the bitter gall, a cup was drained,
yet still we sit and sup.

The memory slashed wide open,
the gaping dying flesh,
a sacrificial action by which we all are blessed?

Much better to
remember the height
and depth of love,

a hand reached out in
healing,

a touch?
a tear?

a whisper?

Yes!

That undying love!

The sky at sunset, bleeding

Is all grace gone?

When the sky at sunset, bleeding,
mirrors pain that fells our hope;
it seems that love is fast receding,
sowing tears that can't be quelled.
Can it be that God, seceding,
leaves this world, all grace expelled?

When the streets are warm with terror,
as emotions run or seize,
singing notes of music shudder,
when God's tempo should relieve,
must we lose the spirit's rudder, losing hope?
We start to grieve.

When the darkness is descending,
night a quiet, yet chilling, shroud,
folding round us bleak, unending,
muting what we cry aloud,
is God near, with grace transcending
fear and dread, defeat or cloud?

55

BEING MORTAL

Things we know are never wholly certain

Things we know are never wholly certain,
we fathom and explore,
we test the tangled evidence
while seeking to decide.
This is the time of crisis,
of decision,
a time for making choices.
Life sometimes stutters,
moving on in stages.
At others it seems seldom interrupted.
Day to day passes without incident.

Then the cancer, infarction,
crippling us with indecision.
Death is inevitable since our birth.
But should we, as the poet wrote…
"strive against the dying of the light"?

Or, windhover like, roll,
riding on the steady air,
swing in mastery
of this fluid existence?

Broken pinioned we may
plummet,
God forbid.
But is it worth the struggle?
To claw heavenward,
perhaps survive,
at what present cost?
And all that now determines
action will sound ephemeral,
of little consequence.

Such impulses drive the
decisions we will make,
for life or death,
in love or grace.

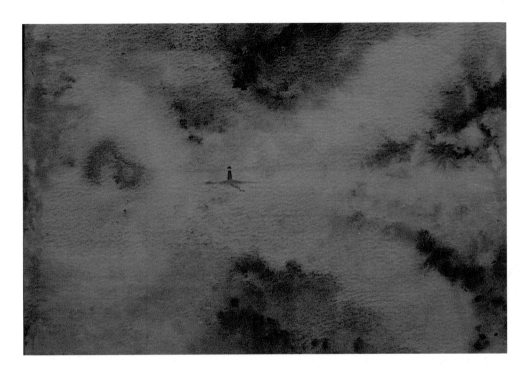

For life or death?

Hugging my shoulders

Hugging my shoulders to myself,
small, vulnerable as a child,
I'm held again, aged three or four.
A grazed knee?
Or did someone shout?
A nightmare,
waking in the darkness?

Growing, still vulnerable,
sticks and stones never near,
but words?
Teasing?
Smallness?
Isolation. Friends were hard to make.
Easy to lose.

Alone again, naturally,
not trusting loyalty,
three's a crowd,
shielded by humour.
Hurt by broken trust and an
inability to trust even myself.

So let the logos weave its way,
the words I knit together fold a
blanket round me,
imaginary.
Hugging my shoulders,
small, vulnerable,
waiting for death.

Loneliness is a passing place

Loneliness is a passing place,
a place to rest along the way.
Loneliness is a place to leave
but sometimes here we stop and stay.

I know the keeper of a light
that flares the sky, that scans the night;
the light is trimmed and by its beam
sleek boats skim quietly, safe, unseen;
but he is lonely, by that light
he finds life lonely, day or night.

Loneliness is a passing place,
a place to rest along the way…
Loneliness is a place to leave
but sometimes here to stop and stay.

I knew the loneliness he felt
beneath the skies, across the sea;
for from that lonely wooden tower
I sensed a shadow watching me…

Loneliness is a passing place,
But here I sheltered from the swell
Here was the place, the place to be,
the place that I would harbour well.

Jesus was a sailor (after Leonard Cohen)

AGEING

Is this the day that dawns today (A reflection on Coronavirus inspired by thoughts of Simon Sutcliffe)

Is this the day that dawns today, when all the world stands still,
when human lives are challenged in their arrogant, self-will?
Is this a time to sound again the grace, which from our youth,
has brought us to this point in time to face eternal truth?
We wonder at the rhythms of creation we observe,
the genesis of all we see, the laws we sense and serve,
yet, when we read in scripture of the wonders of this course,
we tend to shut our eyes to one last day of rest at source.

Now is the moment action takes the place of hollow sighs,
the sighs that speak of emptiness, of loneliness and lies;
great God, within this Sabbath rest we question and explore,
is this a time when you recede, a tide drawn from the shore?
Now is a time of deep compassion, caring and concern,
when every person needs the love that money cannot earn.
This is a time when values shift and search for solid ground,
to put aside our selfishness to go where grace is found.

Moonlight over fields

On and on

On and on
petals unfold.

Sap drives the green fuse beyond darkness;
babies bawl and grasp at breath,
thrust into the world.

Glimpsing light, elbowing space,
reaching for the now
that's not yet.

Life struggles with its own.

Under the blue canopy we
grow together.
Here we lust and laugh,
praise and die together.

Then,
earth to earth,
     ashes to ashes
          dust to dust

on … and on … and on …

Slow sailing*

In age, so often, life, it seems,
is like a leaky boat.
Our forward progress slows and swings
with the tide,
its ebb and flow.

For want of caulking,
bilges seep and timbers creak
with every swing and turn,
but still we cut between the waves,
while tacking with the flow.

And though it may seem strange
to some
who wish to race ahead,
the more I travel now, I think,
I'd rather travel slow.

The harbour will come soon
enough,
to moor and come to rest,
for now a passage,
calm and slow,
would seem much better blessed.

* In response to an email from Claire Wilson
(Pastoral Officer of the Hymn Society)

Slow sailing

Such misery is brought by memory

Such misery is brought by memory and all that we anticipate;
such fear is wrought of comprehension.
And of hate?

Tomorrow brings the consummation
of the past,
lost love,
and all that will not last.

Quietus;

yet not so quiet,
nor restful,
as I wait a strumming dawn.

*I give to this land, and the land to me**

I give to this land, and the land to me,
that down millennia God has graced:

Here in the depth of this hollow oak
the satin grain, the thorn-less wood,

this hall of God, this belfry tower
the holly's way beyond the font,

through death and suffering,
through re-birth
to Christ, to God, to all.

*To Alan Garner, a Cheshire author

Cheshire Oak

We cannot see the future

We cannot see the future,
nor live as in the past,
our time the present moment,
yet know this will not last.
But can a human construct
give answers or make sense
as everyone will struggle
with this, the present tense?

Our understanding staggers,
but what can history prove?
What scripture has a message
to help us rest or move?
The wilderness was testing
a place to learn and think,
a sudden unthought action
might push us to the brink.

So in this present moment
the greatest gift is time,
a time of recollection
before life's upward climb.
And can our faith sustain us?
Or simple human love?
While waiting in the valley
we lift our eyes above.

The heavens will not answer,
but through each silent night
the stars might make us wonder
at their insistent light.
We live within an instant,
as finite as our breath,
suspended in a moment
between our life and death.

What matters in this moment
is how we love and live,
is how we treat each other,
of how we share and give;
to speculate is pointless,
this is the earth we know,
this edifice of living:
what will OUR loving show?

Going home